CTBI LENT COURSE 2006

Easter People
in a Good Friday World

WITNESSING CHRIST IN THE CONFLICT OF LIFE

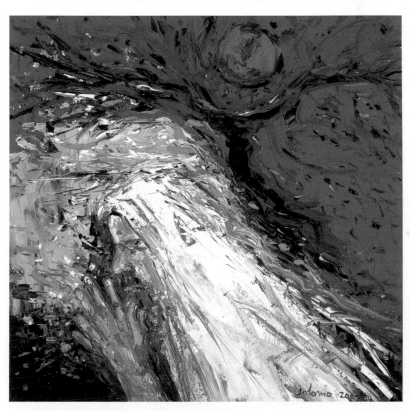

First published in 2006 by the
Churches Together in Britain and Ireland

Bastille Court
2 Paris Garden
London SE1 8ND

info@ctbi.org.uk
www.ctbi.org.uk

ISBN 0 85169 327 X

Line drawings by Nial Smith Design
Layout and cover design by Heather Macpherson

Contents

Foreword

A WORD FROM THE CTBI PRESIDENTS:

The Ecumenical Lent Course for 2006 is part of a regular and very widely supported movement in cities, towns, and villages across these islands. In many places, Christians of different traditions meet in small groups, often in homes, to reflect together on shared issues of faith and life. In these meetings, prejudices are overcome, and friendships begin or continue to deepen. The tens of thousands of Christians who meet together in these 'small Christian communities' find for themselves that "more unites us than divides us". Often these meetings provide the contacts and inspiration which bear fruit in local initiatives of various kinds.

In contrast to our ecumenical bridge-building, the first few years of the third Christian millennium have revealed that violence in a variety of manifestations is an issue in the world and in and for the Churches. War, terrorist attacks, civil wars, crime and violence in local communities, violence and abuse in families, all raise their challenges to the Gospel of Peace and to the followers of the Prince of Peace. As Christians, we dare not turn away from the agonies of the world, because it was by violence that Christ was put to death.

Easter People in a Good Friday World, the CTBI Lent course for 2006, engages with anger, violence, and patterns of Christian response as we seek to live as "Easter People", a phrase of the late Pope John Paul II. Week by week we shall be reflecting on Christ's passion and the world's passion. This course has come out of a process in which CTBI has engaged with the World Council of Churches' Ecumenical Decade to Overcome Violence, 2001 - 2010. We hope that as the fruit of your shared reflection during Lent, you will feel encouraged and better equipped to be peacemakers and reconcilers where you are called to live out your individual and shared discipleship.

Most Revd Mario Conti, Catholic Archbishop of Glasgow
Revd David Kerr, Methodist Church in Ireland
Revd Nezlin Sterling, New Testament Assembly
Sr Eluned Williams, Methodist Church in Wales
Rt Revd Tom Butler, Bishop of Southwark

Most Revd Mario Conti

Revd David Kerr

Revd Nezlin Sterling

Rt Revd Tom Butler

Sister Eluned Williams

* Acting during a vacancy in the See of York, whose archbishop normally serves as president.

Introduction

Violence in our society, in our lives, is all-pervasive. We are all damaged by it. We *see* the suffering and damage inflicted daily by physical violence of person on person, tribe on tribe, nation on nation; psychological violence by those who wish to dominate and diminish others; and the structural violence of poverty, lack of healthcare, education and social support. Much of our practical Christian witness is to do with helping to heal the wounds of these forms of violence.

In 1998 the World Council of Churches called on the Churches, ecumenical groups and all people of goodwill to go much further. At the end of what is widely regarded as the most violent century in human history, the Churches called for us to work together to overcome violence through peace and justice.
 "We are challenged by a vision of a church, the people of God on the way together, confronting all divisions of race, gender, age or culture, striving to realise justice and peace, upholding the integrity of creation".
They declared the years 2001-2010 the World Council of Churches' Decade to Overcome Violence.

Such a radical call presents a profound challenge to us at every level of our personal, family, community and international lives. It requires us firstly to recognize that we live in a culture of violence, that we regard this as normal and assume it to be unchangeable. Secondly, it reminds us that Jesus Christ took on this challenge and offered us through his teaching and example, not only a way of living differently, but a vision of God's non violent realm, based on the culture of love and mercy. Jesus lived in a violent world similar to our own, but resisted its seduction. He was hunted, tricked, trapped and killed in ways that we might recognize today. And he confronted his persecutors not by mirroring their behaviour, but with love and forgiveness. He overcame violence and a violent world felt (feels?) threatened by him. As witnesses of Christ, how can we aspire to this example? Are we, as Christians, required to so aspire?

Easter People in a Good Friday World aims to help us explore these issues by looking at aspects of violence through the lens of the Easter story: Jesus' betrayal and arrest; conviction by the temple court without due process; the release of Barabbas instead of Jesus; the humiliation of Jesus by the soldiers; the steadfast role of women in Jesus' ministry, but written out of history; and the witnessed burial of Jesus.

The journey may be difficult for us. It may cause us to re-encounter experiences of suffering violence as a victim, or a perpetrator. *It will require us to be vulnerable and honest.* It may at times be challenging and distressing. But we are not alone on this journey and we know that any suffering we feel is shared.

Easter People in a Good Friday World invites us to name and confront violence in its many forms. It leads us on a dark and downward journey through fear, betrayal, retaliation, victimization, humiliation, rejection, isolation and denial – each step with Jesus to his death. It is the story of human rejection of God's way. The study pack ends there, but the story doesn't. Nor should we.

> "Peace I leave with you; my peace I give to you; not as the world gives do I give to you"
>
> John 14.27

Steve Whiting
Religious Society of Friends (Quakers)

Easter People in a Good Friday World

Using this material

This Lent course has been inspired by the churches' Decade to
Overcome Violence; the sessions are designed as a complementary
exploration of the theme of violence within the passion narrative.
They are meant for use alongside the meditation and reflection on the
passion narrative taking place within a congregation's regular worship
life during this period of Lent. They are not an alternative
interpretation of the passion narrative in all its depth and richness.
Devotional material is included in each session so that the material
can became part of your preparation for Easter.

Given the subject under discussion, it will be important for all in the
study group, and particularly the group leader, to be sensitive to the
awakening of potentially painful experiences. Attention should be
paid from the outset to establishing caring and supportive bonds
between group members. Space should be given for emotions to be
expressed.

Try to work in groups of between 5 and 11 whenever possible. If this can't be arranged, don't worry – just work with the numbers you do have. No two groups will be the same (just as no two people are the same) so it is important that you adapt the material in each session to suit your group.

Group members should listen attentively to the insights and experiences of others as well as being ready to offer their own. Whilst a trusting and supportive environment is desirable, all should keep aware that the study programme is to help us discern God's purpose for us in a violent world. Each is responsible for themselves as well as for others. Clear boundaries may have to be agreed if the needs of individuals threaten to pull the group in a different direction, and leaders should be sensitive to the need for all to have space to speak, encouraging where appropriate contributions from the less vocal. Additional support for those who require it may be arranged outside the group sessions.

It may be important for some to know the time commitment necessary for the group meetings, so agreement on a start and end time would be helpful from the outset.

Perhaps a Group Agreement could be made from the outset to address some of these issues. It might include, for example, agreed guidelines on confidentiality, speaking only from personal experience, no interruptions, responsibility to listen to others as well as contribute ourselves. These could be written up, displayed at each meeting and gently referred to on occasions when it's felt that an agreement is being broken.

The meetings

Easter People in a Good Friday World contains five sessions. Most groups would wish to study one session per meeting, so in order to complete all five, each group will need to meet five times (we would suggest once a week for five weeks). It is important to work out well in advance when and where the group is to meet so that everyone can put dates, times and venues in their diaries.

The contents of each session

Each session in *Easter People in a Good Friday World* offers a range of material for the group to use. Each session will include:

- a prayer to begin

- a Bible reading (from the New Revised Standard Version)

- some comments on the Bible passage

- resource material on a particular aspect of violence

- some story material from a variety of contexts and places, saying something about building peace, seeking to respond to the issues of violence in our society highlighted by the passion narrative

- questions about the Bible passage and group members' experience

- worship material at the end

Getting started

It is important that group members spend some time at the beginning of each session chatting and getting to know each other - building relationships.

The material in this part of the session is designed to be a starter to the group discussion. It would be good to ask members of the group to think about the questions for themselves for a few moments and then to share their thoughts with the person next to them.
Allow about 15 minutes for this exercise.

Purpose

Each session has a stated purpose and it is important for the group to know this before they begin.
This should take no more than five minutes.

Bible passage

Consider how best to read the Bible passage - should one person read it all? If there is speech, should different people read the different characters? Try to make sure that it is shared together in the most arresting way possible.

Immediately following the Bible passage you'll find **some thoughts about the passage** and we suggest that this should be read by a number of different people, perhaps one per paragraph.
Allow about 25 minutes for this part of the session.

Stories and questions

Read the stories together and then spend some time focusing on the questions following them. These will relate to the stories but also to the theme of the study; we hope that the discussion stimulated by the questions will help group members to think about any practical steps that they can take.
Again, allow about 25 minutes for this part of the session.

Background information

In most sessions you will find some extra resource material (relevant to the subject matter) included in text boxes. This is designed as further information on the issue under discussion. People may agree or disagree with this material, but it is important that the group's time is not taken up in unnecessary discussion – it is not the main focus of the study and may be of limited use. The background information may be read aloud in the group, alternatively individuals might be asked to consider it quietly.

Closing the session

It would be good for the group to pray together (using the suggested symbolic action) about the matters that have been discussed, and then to use the *Easter People in a Good Friday World* affirmation. If the group would enjoy it, then choose a suitable hymn or song to sing as well.

This may take up to 15 minutes.

Timings

The time allocations above for each part of the session allow one hour and twenty five minutes for the group to work together. With time for coffee before and/or after the work that should mean a meeting of about two hours.

If the group needs to meet for less time then do cut down on the time allowed for each section; it will, however, be very difficult to do the exercises effectively in less than one hour. The minimum time for the working session should be one hour and fifteen minutes.

Sensitivity

Many people have some experience of violence of one sort or another in their lives and taking part in these sessions may raise painful issues for them. Group leaders should take the time to read the pastoral material (included on pp.7-8) in order to enable them to deal with these issues in the best possible way.

It is always important to remember when working with groups that different people will react in different ways if confronting painful issues and experiences. Try to make the group as safe an environment as possible for the members. However, it is good to encourage them to share only what they would be comfortable sharing in a group whose purpose is to explore themes rather than to offer counselling.

Nonetheless, sometimes people will be affected in a way that they are not expecting. This will need careful and gentle handling by the leader and group members, and possible referral to a pastoral leader or other suitable qualified persons.

Session I
Be angry, be violent?

Blessed are the peacemakers, for they will be called the children of God.

Matthew 5.9

As you begin:

Take a few moments to start to get to know each other. Go round the group and ask members to introduce themselves giving their name and church and two things that they would like other members of the group to know about them. It is important for group members to think carefully about what they want to say here - what is shared should not be too personal or too threatening.

When everyone has had an opportunity to do this then the group is ready to begin the first session with prayer.

Prayer:

> God of all seasons,
> in your pattern of things,
> there is a time for keeping
> and a time for losing,
> a time for building up
> and a time for pulling down.
> In this holy season of Lent,
> as we journey with our Lord to the cross,
> help us to discern in our lives
> what we must lay down
> and what we must take up;
> what we must end
> and what we must begin.
> Give us grace to lead a disciplined life,
> in glad obedience
> and with the joy

which comes from a closer walk with Christ.

Amen

Book of Common Order, St Andrew Press

Purpose

In this first session we are going to begin to think about anger and
violence and how people's reaction to different situations can lead to
some people acting violently and not others. Through stories, we will
consider how violence can be managed and prevented.

To think about and discuss

Take a few moments to consider the following questions for yourself,
in order to share your reactions with the group.

What makes you really angry? Different things will be appropriate for
different people. Try to come up with examples. What effect does this
anger or fury have on your behaviour?

What do you think anger is? What is righteous anger? Do your
feelings of anger sometimes become feelings of violence, or translate
into actual violence? What happens?

Bible passage

The arrest of Jesus

Read this passage aloud.

Immediately, while he was still speaking, Judas, one of the twelve, arrived; and with him there was a crowd with swords and clubs, from the chief priests, the scribes, and the elders. Now the betrayer had given them a sign, saying, "The one I will kiss is the man; arrest him and lead him away under guard." So when he came, he went up to him at once and said, "Rabbi!" and kissed him. Then they laid hands on him and arrested him. But one of those who stood near drew his sword and struck the slave of the high priest, cutting off his ear. Then Jesus said to them, "Have you come out with swords and clubs to arrest me as though I were a bandit? Day after day I was with you in the temple teaching, and you did not arrest me. But let the scriptures be fulfilled." All of them deserted him and fled.

Mark 14.43-50

Discuss together

- How does this passage make you feel?

- Where is there violence in this passage? What form does it take?

- How did Jesus respond to the violence here?

Some thoughts about the passage

It would be good to read this aloud in the group and it might be helpful to ask different people to read a paragraph each.

When people are under threat it seems to be a common reaction to resort to violence. Just take a look at local and national newspapers or listen to the news; there are always lots of stories that make it clear that even in the twenty-first century, people still get into fights when they feel offended or threatened.

So, it's not very surprising to read that Jesus' arrest was resisted with violence. The different gospel accounts of the event give us slightly different information about who was responsible for the violence. Mark's Gospel tells us that it was someone who stood by. Matthew suggests that it was someone with Jesus (Matt. 26.51) but John named him as Peter (John 18.10).

We are not completely sure about why Jesus' followers had weapons in this passage. Could it be that his followers always carried weapons? Perhaps it was for protection against the robbers who often attacked travellers in the remote places on their journeys. Or could it be that they did not usually carry swords but had brought them along this time because of a sense of impending disaster?

From reading this passage, from our own experience and the stories that we hear all around us, it would appear that violence is an instinctive reaction rather than a more peaceful option when dealing with our enemies. As Jesus reminded those who came to arrest him, they had had plenty of opportunities to do so peacefully, yet they came heavily armed. Why? It might be that understanding the way the authorities in Jerusalem reacted will help us understand the way some in authority act today. Is there something in all of us that means that we sometimes go too far - even when using the rules? Is there something that means that we feel the need to humiliate and crush people?

Violent instincts, whatever their roots, raise questions about how to manage conflict at all levels: personal, in your community, national and international. Wherever violence comes from, its results need to be recognized and managed. In all spheres of life people are beginning to work together to develop methods of conflict management.

ANGER MANAGEMENT - 'THE FINAL STRAW'

Serious conflict can start with something very trivial and escalate. There are always presenting issues when things go wrong. For example when resentment has been smouldering for a long time because someone has not felt listened to; or when anger has been suppressed, or the cause not properly addressed.

We can function for a long time on different levels, presenting a front, which seems united. We can be efficient at work while experiencing stress in other areas of life. But only for so long. Sooner or later the pot boils over and a very trivial incident can assume huge proportions, escalating out of control so that before we know it we cannot resolve it.

(*Journeying through Conflict - part of life* - Baptist Training Pack: Handling Tensions in Church Relationships - Vivienne Lassetter and Ernie Whalley)

ANGER MANAGEMENT AND CHILDREN

A six year old boy tells this story:

    My brother said I hit him

    but I DIDN'T

    My father growled at me

    I got mad at Dad,

    When I get angry it's like

    I've got a volcano in my tummy

The anger management book for children (inspired by this story) seeks to help children understand that words and behaviours which hurt others or ourselves are abusive; that abuse is behaviour, not emotion. As children begin to distinguish the difference between feeling angry (which is OK) and abusive behaviour (which is not OK) so they learn that anger is a healthy emotion when it protects and motivates us ; but when it is bottled up, it can become explosive, depressive and bad for health.

(*A Volcano in my Tummy - Helping children to handle anger*, Elaine Whitehouse and Warick Pudney)

Conflict management

When we "stick to our guns" - hold to our positions - it is
hard to find a way forward. Imagine four people trying to move
a piano to an upstairs room. It gets stuck. What do they do?
For there to be a movement forward (or upwards) each person
needs to make adjustments. In conflict transformation, it is
important to explore interests in order to move beyond
positions.

How then might we move from positions to interests?
Imagine an orange. Two people want it and they want it now.
There is only one orange. What is to happen? Explore the
options: e.g.:
  - cut it in half (compromise)
  - toss a coin (chance)
  - buy another one (expand resources)

But we could ask: What do both want the orange for?
One response might be "I need the rind to make a cake" while
the other response might be: "I need the inside to extract the
juice." Here both can have what they each want. They have
moved from positions to interests and have achieved a win-
win situation.

(Mediation UK training manual: *Journeying Through Conflict*
BUGB)

THE SPIRITUALITY OF NON-VIOLENCE

...the efforts of peace-makers should be based on a strong spirituality. This includes the recognition that true peace comes from God and the realisation of God's presence with us; the central place for prayer... the need for silence and meditation to balance the constant clamour of much modern living; the affirmation of human community; crossing barriers of race, culture and creed to express a common deep desire for true peace and justice based on love. These are all part of the spiritual life which will help to overcome violence and build peace.

John Johansen-Berg

Questions for further discussion:

- How do we prevent situations developing where violence may be an instinctive reaction? Think of one or two personal, local or international examples.

- When conflict does happen, how can we manage it in ways that reduce the likelihood of violence? Are there any clues in the Bible passage about how we might manage violence?

- Can you give examples of conflict management in your own life? It might be that you have experience of marriage guidance, or of mediation in the church or at work. What lessons can we learn from these examples about addressing violence and managing conflict?

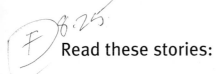

Read these stories:

Marcus Armstrong

Marcus Armstrong was a British volunteer peace mediator on the West Bank. During his second term there he wrote in his journal on day one:

> 'When I was here first time we had forty or so internationals meeting each morning and going out in groups of two/three to do actions and support the local people, last year there were around twenty of us and now there are four, including me. A Swiss, a Canadian, an American and me (there must be a joke in there somewhere). I asked Juda, the American, what they had been doing and he replied with no hint of irony 'we are being friendly but useless' - and I didn't know whether to laugh or cry. And two of them are leaving on Thursday. I am trying to convince myself that we can be of some use in showing solidarity with our presence, bearing witness and sending out reports, but it feels a bit hopeless...'
>
> Marcus Armstrong's journal

Bridging the Gap

> 'Bridging the Gap' is a local community project serving the Gorbals area of Glasgow. It was established in 1998 to enable local churches (Church of Scotland and Roman Catholic) to work together to meet local needs. It aims to work across divides which are apparent in the community, providing opportunities for people to

discover their 'common ground'.

The Gorbals area is served by two secondary schools outside the area, one is Roman Catholic (the largest in Europe) and the other is Non-Denominational, this means pupils need to be bussed from their homes. The transition from primary school to secondary school is a big change for any child but to be thrust into these enormous school communities has proven to be daunting to many of the pupils. Bridging the Gap has initiated a pioneering project to make this transition easier and avoids children experiencing bullying, racism and other forms of violence.

The project is called 'Peer-tutoring'. It uses some of the more troubled pupils in the secondary school as mentors for the incoming primary pupils. This causes them to gain self-respect and take responsibility for others and lessens the incidence of violence and exclusion.

Bridging the Gap, Greyfriars Centre,
Ballater St, Gorbals, Glasgow

These stories are about mediation as presence. They show us how some people are trying to help situations move on simply by being in places of conflict.

- How do you react to these stories? How do they make you feel?

- Where are the places of conflict in your community?

How might you or the churches begin to express your
commitment or solidarity in these places?

- Some of us can go to or spend time in different places,
  near to us, where there is conflict or conflict is being
  prevented. Others may not able to do that but would
  still like to help. In what ways might you be able to
  help in the management of violence and conflict in
  situations that you are aware of?

Bringing the session to a close

Think back to the beginning of the session and what makes you angry.
Take two pieces of paper of equal size. Write the word 'positive' on
one and the word 'negative' on the other. Remember, from the
introductory discussion, the things that make you angry. Where you
feel that the anger is negative or destructive, write it on the piece of
paper headed 'negative'. Where you feel that the anger is creative or
constructive, write it on the piece of paper headed 'positive'.

In a time of prayer, hold in your hand the 'negative' list. Offer prayers
in silence asking God to help you to deal with this anger. Then, tear up
the piece of paper and place the pieces in a basket in the middle of
the room as a symbol of your willingness to let go of the anger.

Then, take the 'creative' or 'positive' list. Commit yourself to using this
anger in positive and constructive ways in the week ahead.

Close with the following affirmation:

Leader: Let us cherish in our hearts that which we proclaim
               with our lips:

All: Goodness is stronger than evil
               Love is stronger than hate
               Light is stronger than darkness
               Truth is stronger than lies.

Session 2:

Punish, repay, reform?

You have heard that it was said, 'An eye for an eye and a tooth for a tooth'. But I say to you, Do not resist an evildoer. But if anyone strikes you on the right cheek, turn the other also...

Matthew 5. 38-39

As you begin:

Take a few moments to introduce any new group members and to
remind each other of your names.
Spend a few minutes thinking back on the previous session and
anything that has stayed with you or struck you since then. Discuss
these things briefly together. Then pray:

Prayer:

> Lord God,
> in this world where goodness and evil
> continue to clash with each other,
> instil in us, and in all your people,
> discernment to see what is right,
> faith to believe what is right;
> and courage to do what is right.
>
> Keep us aware of the subtlety of sin,
> and preserve body, mind, and soul,
> through the power of your Holy Spirit.
> Amen
>
> *Book of Common Order*, St Andrew Press

In the last session we looked at the nature of violence; what makes
people angry and how they respond. We then considered different
ways in which people engage in conflict management and prevention.

Purpose:

In this session we are going to look at how the authorities in Jesus' time perceived and responded to actual and threatened violence. We will also look at how authorities do this today. Through stories we will consider current contrasting approaches to punishment within the criminal justice system.

To think about and discuss:

Why do you think that crime novels and detective stories are so popular? Why do you think there are so many drama series about the police on television? Politicians often talk about whether this reflects or creates public anxiety about crime. Have you ever been a victim of crime? If so, how did it make you feel? How did you feel at the time about the person or people who committed this crime against you? How do you feel now?

7.50 F

High Priest
Jesus.

Bible passage:

Jesus before the Council

Read this passage aloud - you might like to give people different parts to read.

> They took Jesus to the high priest; and all the chief priests, the elders, and the scribes were assembled. Peter had followed him at a distance, right into the courtyard of the high priest; and he was sitting with the guards, warming himself at the fire. Now the chief

priests and the whole council were looking for testimony against Jesus to put him to death; but they found none. For many gave false testimony against him, saying, "We heard him say, 'I will destroy this temple that is made with hands, and in three days I will build another, not made with hands.'" But even on this point their testimony did not agree. Then the high priest stood up before them and asked Jesus, "Have you no answer? What is it that they testify against you?" But he was silent and did not answer. Again the high priest asked him, "Are you the Messiah, the Son of the Blessed One?" Jesus said, "I am; and 'you will see the Son of Man seated at the right hand of the Power' and 'coming with the clouds of heaven.'" Then the high priest tore his clothes and said, "Why do we still need witnesses? You have heard his blasphemy! What is your decision?" All of them condemned him as deserving death. Some began to spit on him, to blindfold him, and to strike him, saying to him, "Prophesy!" The guards also took him over and beat him.

Mark 14.53-65

Discuss together

- Who do you most identify with in this passage? How does it make you feel?

- Where is the violence in this passage? What form does it take?

- What form of justice is operating in this passage?

Some thoughts about the passage

Once again you might like to ask different members of the group to read different paragraphs.

In Mark's Gospel, Jesus, when questioned, agrees that he is the Messiah. Matthew (26.64) and Luke (22.70), have Jesus giving a more enigmatic reply. Matthew's and Luke's Gospels are usually thought to use Mark's Gospel as their main source, so it is interesting that they have a slightly different version. Whether Jesus was condemned by what he said about himself or not, the trial gave his opponents the excuse they needed to have him put to death.

Any judicial system can be abused to achieve the ends of the state. Even when guilt is determined in a just way, there are questions about how we deal with the person convicted and about the purpose of punishment. Is it designed to deter potential offenders by its severity? Is it intended to make society feel good because the person who committed the crime is suffering? Is it a way of reforming the offender? Or, perhaps, it is seen as a mixture of all of these.

Justice can be seen as **retributive** or **restorative**. In retributive justice the emphasis is on the punishment of the offender. In restorative justice, the emphasis is on reforming the offender and enabling them to go some way to righting the wrong they have committed. Restorative justice also attempts to let the victim feel that they have been heard. There are explorations to discover approaches in which the justice system might allow a greater emphasis on restorative justice.

RESTORATIVE JUSTICE

A new approach to crime and punishment

First...

Conventional justice says that people who do wrong should be punished. Restorative justice starts by offering help to the victim, and says that the offender should make amends, either to the victim if he or she wants it, or to the community.

Second...

Offenders are encouraged to accept responsibility and make things right. 'Retribution' literally means paying back; but if, to pay back the harm caused by the offender, we inflict further harm on the offender, we are merely adding to the total amount of harm in the world. In courts offenders have every incentive to deny, or minimize, the harm they caused to the victim, so as to escape, or reduce, their punishment.

Third...

The victim and offender can speak to each other directly, not through lawyers, without the constraints of courtroom rules. The victim can tell the offender the effects of the crime, and ask questions such as 'Why me?' 'Why did you do it?' The offender can explain how it all came about, and usually apologizes. One criminologist, the Norwegian Nils Christie, has said that the professional lawyers, police and social workers have 'stolen' conflicts from their 'owners'; restorative justice gives them back.

Fourth...

Another difference is that restorative justice involves the

community, at several different levels. The original work on restorative justice used trained lay mediators, and this is a strong tradition in restorative justice, although in many places professionals have been brought in. Using volunteers widens the range of people in the community who have met victims and offenders at first hand, giving them a more human understanding of the pressures on offenders as well as the effects on victims. Better still, if the mediators are trained and supervised by an independent voluntary organization, accredited to a national body, the restorative ideal can be maintained and developed independently of the constraints of the state-run system - though inevitably there must be close liaison with it, as well as adequate funding.

HISTORICAL ROOTS

The first American attempt at restorative justice was started in Indiana by a Mennonite, Howard Zehr, who also provided a theoretical base. Starting from the Old Testament, he points out in his book *Changing Lenses* (2nd ed., 1995) that the underlying ideal was shalom, which means not only peace but social well-being, and its root is linked to shillum, paying back. The much-quoted 'an eye for an eye' does not focus on demanding retribution but on limiting it, and in any case was superseded by Jesus: 'but I say, do good to those who harm you'.

Zehr lists ways in which our conventional justice system contrasts with biblical justice, for example:

Contemporary justice	Biblical justice
An inquiry into guilt	A search for solutions
Focus on infliction of pain	Focus on making right
Justice opposed to mercy	Justice based on mercy
Justice as maintenance of status quo	Justice seeking to transform status quo
Focus on guilt and abstract principles	Focus on harm done
Wrong as violation of rules	Wrong as violation of people, relationships, shalom
The state as victim	People, shalom as victim
Justice serves to divide	Justice aims at bringing together

(Martin Wright: *Justice and Peace - a Restorative Response to Crime,* The Bridge, The Southwark Diocesan Newspaper October 2002)

Questions for further discussion

- Think about the patterns of justice that we have now. What kind of justice system would you like us to have? What should its aims be?

- Do any members of the group have any experience of the justice system as a juror, a victim of a crime, or as a witness to a crime, or as someone being prosecuted, or as someone who works within the justice system ? How do you feel about the system? Do you think that you were fairly treated?

• Do you think that there are groups, or do you know of any groups, that suffer disproportionately in the justice system? Why do you think this is?

• Do you think that there are any ways in which we can make sure that there are not miscarriages of justice either because of uninformed popular opinion or the corruption of power. What might we do?

F 6.30

SOME FACTS ABOUT PRISONS:

All the research shows that the men and women in British prisons today are extraordinarily disadvantaged and vulnerable individuals. The Government's Social Exclusion Unit has found that:

Compared with the general population, prisoners are:
thirteen times as likely to have been in care as a child,
thirteen times as likely to have been unemployed,
ten times as likely to have been a regular truant or excluded from school, and
five times more likely to have been in receipt of benefits.

cont.

Half of all prisoners are at or below the level expected of an 11 year old in reading.

Two thirds cannot compete with the average junior school leaver in numeracy and four fifths in writing

These statistics show that it is dangerous to immediately equate criminality with moral degeneracy...where offenders come from broken and impoverished homes, reared in an atmosphere of contempt for the police and the law and whose parents made no serious attempt to keep them in school, the quality of the moral training they received must have been seriously impaired. Rectifying this is one of the roles incumbent on a properly humane prison regime.

(*A Place of Redemption:* the report of the Catholic Bishops' Conference of England and Wales).

GRENDON PRISON

In Grendon Prison the therapeutic experience for the most serious violent and sexual offenders depended upon opportunities they took to educate themselves, increasing their self worth through learning to be accountable and thereby enabling their enormous energy to express itself in positive, artistic and pro-social ways. They apply to join the community because they had reached a point at which they want to alter the pattern of their behaviour and themselves.

cont.

Through brutally honest group sessions and community meetings the men acknowledge and own the reality of the terrible things they have done, while at the same and without turning it into an excuse, they have to recognise that they themselves had been moulded by circumstances that were not in their control. What made the difference, what gave them back their future was the decision to try to take control over their destiny, probably for the first time in their lives. Part of the process involved a radical kind of self-forgiveness that meant accepting the way the universe had formed them. This is dynamic forgiveness in action, but contained the drama of the offender's own life. Creative forgiveness can have a life-changing impact on all the actors in the tragedies of humanity.

Being unable to forgive can end up dominating a whole life or a life of a whole people. We can see this in international affairs as well as in the individual lives of victims.

(Tim Newell, former Governor of Grendon Prison, writing in *Rethinking Sentencing - a contribution to the debate*, Church House Publishing)

Read these stories

Frank Cooke

Frank Cooke's story tells of the rehabilitation of a former "most wanted person" from within the walls of Grendon prison.

Cooke had been incarcerated for over half his life, wreaking havoc in every prison in which he was locked up. One day while in solitary, he was interviewed by Dr Ray Gillet, the medical superintendent of Grendon prison where radical ideas had developed on the rehabilitation of prisoners through psychotherapeutic treatment. But when Cooke was transferred there he continued to cause trouble. One day after he assaulted some members of staff he was summoned to see Dr Gillett. He assumed he would be told that he would be sent back to the harsher regime of the conventional prison. Instead Dr Gillett put his arm around the recidivist's shoulders. Frank Cooke burst into tears... When Frank burst into tears he crossed a threshold of understanding which marks the real beginning of a therapeutic activity. Frank Cooke believes that the corrupted values of his friends and family set him into a criminal career and that his deviancy was confirmed by his experiences of penal institutions before he went to Grendon. But, in his autobiography, he puts his finger on something deeper and far more resonant: "you can't love yourself and go around hurting people. It doesn't work like that," he writes "You hate yourself and that's why you hate everything else." The first person he ever felt love from was Dr Gillett. At the age of 43 having spent all but 16 years of his life in some form of institution he was released from jail. The years that have followed have been far from easy, but thankfully crime free.

(adapted from *A Place of Redemption*: the Report of the Catholic Bishops' Conference of England and Wales)

Myra Hindley

In 1966 Myra Hindley, aged 23, and Ian Brady, aged 27, were jointly charged with the murder of three children. There is little doubt that had this trial taken place before 1965, both the defendants would have been hanged. Two days after the trial ended the judge wrote to the then Home Secretary. 'Though I believe Brady is wicked beyond belief without hope of redemption, (short of a miracle) I cannot feel the same is necessarily true of Hindley once she is removed from his influence. At present she is as deeply corrupted as Brady but it is not so long ago that she was taking instruction in the Roman Catholic Church and was a communicant and a normal sort of girl'. For many years Hindley struggled to be taken seriously as a reformed person... She claimed that she was 'a political prisoner' and described herself as '... a sacrificial victim ...holding the projected hatred, fear and fury of the nation's psyche...the classical scapegoat'.

(from *Sin and Forgiveness* by Kay Carmichael, published by Ashgate Gower House)

The Victim/Offender Reconciliation Programme, Canada

A ... series of offences in Elmira, near Kitchener in Canada - criminal damage by two young men on a drunken spree - led to an unusual response.

A young Mennonite probation officer, Mark Yantzi, suggested that instead of punishment, they might meet their victims and discuss how to make things right. Surprisingly, Judge Gordon McConnell agreed, and Yantzi set off with the young men to visit as many of the 22 victims as could be traced. Some wanted just an apology; others asked the offenders to pay the excess on their insurance claim, or to do community service. The successful experiment became the Victim/ Offender Reconciliation Program (VORP), and the idea spread to America, Britain and other European countries.

Some years later:

Russ Kelly, a mature law student, heard a guest speaker explaining a celebrated local case that had sparked an international movement called "restorative justice." The more she said - about slashed tyres, angry victims and sheepish kids - the more it sunk in that she was talking about him.

He had no idea that one of the worst chapters in his life had since become a textbook example of justice outside the sterile confines of a courtroom. Although it opened his eyes, the experience didn't magically solve everything; it took him years more to finally beat a problem with drugs and booze.

The local paper, the Kitchener-Waterloo Record, reports that Judge McConnell, now retired, serves as a volunteer with VORP - and that Kelly was so impressed by all that has come of his youthful run-in with the law that he signed up for training to become a volunteer himself.

(Martin Wright: *Justice and Peace - a Restorative Response to Crime,* The Bridge , The Southwark Diocesan Newspaper October 2002)

These stories help us to look at restorative justice and the dynamic of forgiveness.

- What is your first reaction to these stories?

- What can they tell us about reform?

- What can they tell us about forgiveness?

- What do you think might bring more offenders to a point where they want to reform themselves?

Bringing the session to a close

Close the session with prayer for those who have been the victims of crime; for those who are in prison and those who administer prisons throughout the world. For those who seek to work for restorative justice and those who seek to forgive and be forgiven.

You might like to take a picture of the Amnesty International Cross (or an actual one, if available) and use this as a way of remembering in your prayers political prisoners around the world.

Close with the following affirmation (used at the end of

each session):

Leader:	Let us cherish in our hearts that which we proclaim with our lips:
All:	Goodness is stronger than evil Love is stronger than hate Light is stronger than darkness Truth is stronger than lies.

Session 3

Forgive, forget?

Father, forgive them; they do not know what they are doing.

Luke 23. 34

As you begin:

Take a few moments to say hello to each other again and make sure that you have remembered everyone's names. Spend some time discussing anything that you have thought about as a result of the last session. Then pray:

Prayer

> Almighty God,
> your Son came to be the Saviour of the world
> and the Prince of peace.
> Give us grace to follow in his ways
> and to fulfil our calling
> as peacemakers in his name.
> May his Holy Spirit
> so move in the hearts of all people
> and among the nations of the world,
> that the barriers of fear, suspicion, and hatred
> which separate us may crumble and fall,
> and the peoples of the world
> be united in justice and peace;
> through Jesus Christ our Lord.
> Amen
>
> *Book of Common Order*, St Andrew Press

In the last session we looked at ways in which courts of law deal with those judged to be a violent threat to society.

Purpose:

In this session we are going to look at situations where people resort to violence to achieve political or religious goals, and what it takes to forgive.

To think about and discuss:

Take a few moments to consider these questions for yourself, in order to share your reactions with the group.

Think of some of the stories of terrorist action that you have seen on the television or read about in the newspaper in the last few weeks. How do you feel about those who have taken this form of action? Are there instances in which you think that violence is justified? Can you explain how you decide what they are? Have you ever felt that violence was the only possibility to solve a situation in which you were involved? Describe the situation. What happened?

Bible passage

The release of Barabbas

Read this passage aloud

> Now at the festival he used to release a prisoner for
> them, anyone for whom they asked. Now a man called
> Barabbas was in prison with the rebels who had
> committed murder during the insurrection. So the crowd
> came and began to ask Pilate to do for them according

to his custom. Then he answered them, "Do you want me to release for you the King of the Jews?" For he realised that it was out of jealousy that the chief priests had handed him over. But the chief priests stirred up the crowd to have him release Barabbas for them instead. Pilate spoke to them again, "Then what do you wish me to do with the man you call the King of the Jews?" They shouted back, "Crucify him!" Pilate asked them, "Why, what evil has he done?" But they shouted all the more, "Crucify him!" So Pilate, wishing to satisfy the crowd, released Barabbas for them; and after flogging Jesus, he handed him over to be crucified.

Mark 15.6-15

Discuss together:

- Who are the characters involved here?

- Why do you think Barabbas was released?

- How do you respond to what happens in this passage?

- What connections, if any, do you find between this scenario and situations which you find in your own context?

Some thoughts about the passage

It would be good to read this aloud in the group and it might be helpful to ask different people to read a paragraph each.

The Romans were holding a group of men in prison after an uprising against the occupation which had resulted in deaths. Some would have seen them as terrorists, others as freedom fighters. Among the prisoners was Barabbas. He was thought by the authorities to be a threat to the state, and was locked up in the interests of national security. Yet, he was used by the authorities as a pawn in a game with the populace.

History shows us that governments can have ambiguous relationships with terrorists. We sometimes discover that governments offer clandestine support for terrorist groups, because it serves their political purpose, even whilst publicly condemning the violence. Terrorists can also provide a useful common enemy against whom society can be united.

The relationship between religion and political violence was present in Jesus' day and in the circumstances around his trial and death. Today, many leaders (self-appointed and elected) claim religious motivation and justification for their violent projects.

Issues around terrorism have always been complex and ambiguous. They raise questions about the use of violence in political conflict; the need to attend to questions of security; the difficulties in defining the enemy; the taking and trading of prisoners and hostages and the role of popular opinion in judic ial rulings.

VIOLENCE AND RELIGION

...Osama bin Laden praised God after 9/11 because he believed that the collapse of the twin towers was God's will. A young Hamas suicide bomber told the video camera that he was 'doing this for Allah'. The 9/11 hijackers believed that they were performing a sacred duty giving glory to God. The Rev. Michael Bray bombs abortion clinics and his friend, Rev. Paul Hill has murdered a pro-abortion doctor and his assistant, because they believe in Dominion Theology. Dominion Theology states that 'Christianity must reassert the dominion of God over all things, including secular politics and society'. The vision of a Christian nation emerging from this theology is in opposition to the moral evils of secular society such as:

abortion on demand, fornication, homosexuality, sexual entertainment, state ursurption of parental rights and God-given liberties, statist-collectivist theft from citizens through devaluation of their money and redistribution of their wealth, and evolutionism taught as a monopoly viewpoint in public schools.

Timothy McVeigh, the Oklahoma bomber was also influenced by Dominion and Reconstructionist Theology, the latter strongly emphasising the creation of a theocratic state. The Western media persists in speaking about Islamic terrorists but never Christian terrorists. And yet Christians in Indonesia have justified and supported excessive paramilitary violence. There is a Christian paramilitary force called the '*Black Bats*' who '*are said to be responsible for the abduction of children and the mutilation of hundreds of Muslims and yet they are revered by the local Christians who see them as defenders of their ancestral lands*'.

Radovan Karadzic and Ratko Mladic are wanted for war crimes committed in Kosovo. (Some) Orthodox church leaders have honoured them as '*chosen to follow the thorny path of Christ*' while Karadzic has been decorated by the Greek Orthodox Church as '*one of the most prominent sons of our Lord Jesus Christ working for peace*'.

So there is Christian terrorism carried out in some cases by clergy and in others legitimised and blessed by the church and its leaders. It is easy to dismiss this as extreme and yet the people who do these things in the name of God or Allah are often decent people. Mark Juergensmayer who interviewed Rev Mike Bray said, '*I found nothing sinister or intensely fanatical about him. He was a cheerful, charming, handsome man in his early 40s who liked to be called Mike*'. But Juergensmayer's global research shows '*how religious ideas and the sense of religious community has been endemic to the cultures of violence from which terrorism has sprung*'. There is some odd attraction between religion and violence, some causal connection between the two.

Fundamentalism is a growing part of religious reality and it appears to be the mindset of those who find justification for their use of violence in their religious beliefs or vision. It has been described as *'a historically recurring tendency within Judeo-Christian-Muslim religious traditions'* and *'as an authoritarian reaction to the fear of chaos evoked by postmodernism and globalisation'*.

(Johnston McMaster at the CTBI Conference *Beyond Violence* (2004) Swanwick)

Questions for further discussion:

- Terrorism is usually thought of as committed by small groups of people who are reacting against something. Do you think that there is a moral difference between acts of violence committed by terrorist groups and acts of violence committed by states? Try to describe the difference.

- In the Bible passage what do you think the difference is between Pilate and Barrabas?

- Do you think that there is a difference between the actions of a suicide bomber and a martyr?

THE ART OF FORGIVENESS

Forgiveness is not an act of putting the past behind, forgetting, it is not an act of amnesia, but a process whereby perpetrator and victim can set each other free to live the future in a way that the scars of the past will no longer bind or hold back.

'Evil acts create chains that lock perpetrators and victims together... An act of forgiveness needs to be understood as a complex process of unlocking painful bondage, of mutual liberation.'

(From *The Art of Forgiveness*, Geiko Muller-Fahrenholz, World Council of Churches)

Read these stories

Victim support ... a cautionary tale

Colette is the Personal Development Facilitator employed by the Methodist Church to serve the churches ecumenically in Merseyside. Her role is to assist and support survivors of sexual abuse and to enable ministers and congregations to understand the issues involved including helping them to see the most appropriate ways by which they might support survivors. 'Many people,' says Colette 'feel out of their depth, or else fail to appreciate the cost in time and energy involved in giving victims the support they need'. As well as committing time to be with victims, good support is dependant on people having effective listening skills. Developing good listening skills amongst ministers and congregations is central to Colette's work.

Colette is herself a survivor of abuse. She creates time and space to hear what survivors want to say including what they are not permitted to say in other situations. Many she notes 'come feeling that their trauma has taken over their world, it seems there are no boundaries, every part of their life is affected and invaded'. Their expectation born out of bitter previous experiences is that the person listening will do nothing about what they are told. They want rescuing and it doesn't happen. Colette and others engaged in this support role, however, are clear that they are not there to rescue, but to empower survivors to develop the skills within themselves to make things better. Naturally feelings of exhaustion and confusion mean the victims resist this idea at first ...but with time...a lot of time... they can begin to see change in their situation and to believe again in themselves.

Colette has many stories of women who have been further damaged by churches dispensing forgiveness like cheap pills and exhorting victims (without reference to context and circumstances) to forgive seventy times seven. She also has stories of churches who have taken survivors seriously, who know that forgiveness without repentance is cheap grace. Survivors need to know that they have the right to expect and to see tangible signs of remorse and of change in a person's life before there can be any reasonable expectation of forgiveness. Graffiti signs on the wall of a Merseyside church hall read "f..k forgiveness". This, says Colette, is the honest sentiment of many who are abused and not believed. Rather than be shocked the church needs to comprehend the depth of the pain that leaves people with these emotions. 'When you are in a life of abuse hard words may not be nice but they reflect the reality'...compassion goes beyond words, entering into the struggle and empathizing with the pain of those whose experience defies expression.

(From an interview - used with Colette's permission)

'I was part of it. I killed your father'

Different group members could each be asked to read the part of the different characters in this interview: Simon Fanshawe - the interviewer (SF); Jo Berry - whose father was killed in the Brighton bombing in 1984 (JB) and Patrick Magee - who was convicted for planting the Brighton bomb (PM).)

Twenty years after the Brighton bomb, the IRA man responsible and the daughter of one of the victims came together in an extraordinary meeting. Simon Fanshawe took the chair.

JB: Do you remember the moment when you stopped being there to justify and opened up? Because you actually stopped talking.

PM: I do. I had this political hat on my head ... the need to explain. But then I had to confront something that I have to confront every tIme I meet you and perhaps more so now because of where we are and the day it is, and that is that I am sitting with someone whose father I killed. Here in Brighton. Twenty years after your father's death. I do not shirk my responsibilities for that. It was an IRA action, but whatever the political justification for it, I was part of it and I killed your father. And every time I meet you that is at the forefront of my mind. It is full of profundity and it's shattering. Quite honestly, there's no hiding to be done behind politics. The rehearsed arguments and the line might be sincere, but it's inappropriate. We were communicating as two human beings.

SF: What was the sign to you, Jo, that Pat had opened up?

JB: That political hat came off and I think, Patrick, you took your glasses off; there was a tear. And you said, "I have never met anyone so open, with such dignity" - is that what you said? You said to me, "I want to hear your anger, I want to hear your pain." And that is when I knew that we were going on a journey. That this was not going to be one meeting. And as you say, we were meeting as two human beings. My need to meet you matched your need to meet me. I did not expect that because I heard from other ex-prisoners who said to me, "Jo, you may need to meet Patrick, but he doesn't need to meet you."

But together we opened up your commitment to hear even my most difficult feelings. You have never shirked away from the times when I have been really angry or hurt or frustrated or cried. You heard it.

PM: If anything, that was a relief to me. It is probably harder when someone who I have hurt is prepared to listen and try to understand. Dealing with anger almost seems easier in some way. If that makes sense to anybody. I'm not sure it makes sense to me.

SF: What have you both got out of it?

JB: It is not easy, for either of us. I think we both have been courageous to meet and that courage has carried on. I am not an easy option for Pat. When Pat talks about the other choices not being there, not just in Ireland but around the world, that helps me understand why people resort to violence. It makes my passion stronger to find other choices. That is what this is about. Nothing is going to bring my dad back. Caring for Pat makes it easier to get some of my humanity back.

PM: The big lesson is that if you see people as human beings, how can you possibly hurt them? Then you think of all the barriers to that simple relationship occurring - political, social, economic. When people are marginalised or excluded they are left only with their anger. So do everything to remove the blocks and let people be human with each other. That's the lesson from my meeting Jo.

SF: Is there something that you'd like to say to each other that you feel would be important for people to hear?

PM: I was talking about how tough it is - and it is tough we both know that - to meet you. But also I know I will keep on meeting you as long as you're prepared to meet me. And I thank you, Jo, for being prepared to be as open as you are to me after what I did to you.

JB: I appreciate that. (Pause). For me, meeting you today, 20 years after you planted the bomb that killed my father, is part of something I have yearned for and worked hard for. It has taken years to reach this point, where I can sit with you and listen and understand. It means so much to me. I feel us being together brings something positive out of what happened 20 years ago. Every time we meet you are more open and vulnerable. And on days like this I really appreciate that.

(Transcript of an interview printed in *The Guardian*, Wednesday, October 13th 2004)

These interviews can help us to see the real difficulties in trying to understand situations and to respond to them in a way that will help to bring about an end of violence rather than perpetuating it.

- How do you react to these stories? How do they make you feel?

- How do you think that you would react if you were asked to forgive those who had harmed you or your family?

- How do you think forgiveness happens? Do you think that there could be times when it is not appropriate to forgive?

- What do you think forgiveness is?

- Do you think that forgiveness is a necessary starting point for peace?

Bringing the session to a close

You might like to use a world map to pray for peace:

Place a large map of the world on the floor. Ask people to think about places in the world where fragile and risky peace processes are underway. Invite group members to place a lighted candle and say a prayer for the peace process in the place where they have put their candle.

Remember, too, the different world religions, that separately and together they may be a growing source and inspiration for peace and reconciliation. Also remember places where individuals, communities and nations seek to come to terms with the past and to build a new future.

Close with the following affirmation:

Leader: Let us cherish in our hearts that which we proclaim with our lips:

All: Goodness is stronger than evil
Love is stronger than hate
Light is stronger than darkness
Truth is stronger than lies.

Session 4

Losing our humanity?

Do not think that I have come to bring peace to the earth; I have not come to bring peace, but a sword.

Matthew 10. 34

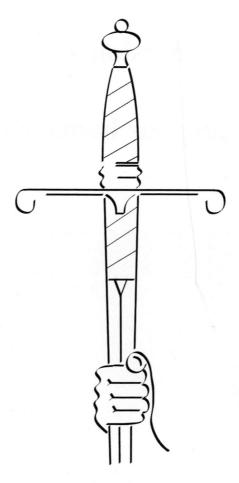

A 7.30

As you begin:

Greet one other and take a few moments to reflect on any thoughts that you have had sInce the last session on forgiveness and being forgiven. Then pray:

Prayer

> Saviour of the world,
> though easier paths beckoned
> and friends pleaded for you to stay with them,
> you turned your face resolutely
> towards Jerusalem,
> determined to go all the way to Calvary.
> Take us with you now, Lord,
> and show us how through your sufferings
> violence and evil are conquered and the world is saved.
> Amen
>
> *Book of Common Order*, St Andrew Press

In the last session we looked at violence as a means to an end. Then we looked at what it takes for victims and perpetrators of violence to be forgiven.

Purpose

In this session we will consider the de-humanizing effect violence has on both perpetrators and victims and begin to consider how the effects of violence can be healed.

To think about and discuss

Have you, or has someone you know, ever felt victimized? What happened?

Have you ever been in a situation where you have done something simply because you were part of a crowd? How did it feel then? How do you feel about it now?

Bible passage:

The soldiers mock Jesus

Read this passage aloud

Then the soldiers led him into the courtyard of the palace (that is, the governor's headquarters); and they called together the whole cohort. And they clothed him in a purple cloak; and after twisting some thorns into a crown, they put it on him. And they began saluting him, "Hail, King of the Jews!" They struck his head with a reed, spat upon him, and knelt down in homage to him. After mocking him, they stripped him of the purple cloak and put his own clothes on him. Then they led him out to crucify him.

When it was noon, darkness came over the whole land until three in the afternoon. At three o'clock Jesus cried out with a loud voice, "Eloi, Eloi, lema sabachthani?" which means, "My God, my God, why have you forsaken me?" When some of the bystanders heard it, they said,

"Listen, he is calling for Elijah." And someone ran, filled a sponge with sour wine, put it on a stick, and gave it to him to drink, saying, "Wait, let us see whether Elijah will come to take him down." Then Jesus gave a loud cry and breathed his last. And the curtain of the temple was torn in two, from top to bottom. Now when the centurion, who stood facing him, saw that in this way he breathed his last, he said, "Truly this man was God's Son!"

Mark 15.16-20; 33-39

Discuss together:

- Who are the characters involved here?

- What happens in this passage?

- What sort of violence is taking place here?

- What reactions and responses to the violence do you note?

- What connections, if any, do you find here with your own experience of violence, or the violence that you see around you, in society?

- Where can you find God in this passage?

Some thoughts about the passage

It would be good to read this aloud in the group and it might be helpful to ask different people to read a paragraph each.

This part of the passion narrative raises questions about what makes violence acceptable to the perpetrators. The soldiers could have had no animosity against Jesus personally. Their cruel play demonstrates that they didn't think of him as a political threat. They did not see him as a person. The soldiers were not uniquely awful human beings. They demonstrate what can happen when we stop recognizing the humanity of others. This is not a story from a more barbaric age because we know that captors can still do such things to their prisoners. Among other incidences of street violence today we can see that some find it gratifying to give individuals from minority groups 'a good kicking' because 'they don't belong here'.

It seems to be a common feature of many societies that people choose easily identifiable groups of those who are different to blame for their own problems. If you look different, speak a different language or practise a different religion, it is very easy to find yourself being made a scapegoat for everything that goes wrong in your host society.

Once we see people as other than us because they come from a different ethnic, racial or religious group, it is very easy to move to forgetting that they too are human beings. How could the soldiers play degrading and humiliating games with Jesus? How could they take casual enjoyment in violence against him?

At the end of the passage we see the soldier confess that Jesus is the Son of God. What is it about this moment of Jesus' forsakenness which makes it also the moment of revelation for the soldier?

SCAPEGOATING AND VIOLENCE: A DEFINITION

Scapegoating (or witch hunting) is the process of passionately searching for and eliminating agents believed to be causing harm to individuals and groups. By passing the blame for their afflictions onto others, people are able to conveniently distract themselves from the real causes and the efforts they must make to remove them.

Individuals and groups displace their fears of the unknown and their aggression onto groups or individuals that are visible, relatively powerless, and already disliked or stigmatised.

The greater or more intense the chaos and consequent fear of the unknown, the more frequent and persistent is the scapegoating.

The extent of violence involved in scapegoating depends on what the dominant culture legitimises.

Shame, envy, jealousy, and fear are among the powerful emotions behind scapegoating.

(Gerald A. Arbuckle *Violence, Society, and the Church,* Liturgical Press, Minnesota)

Questions for further discussion:

- When people are confronted with those who are different to them they sometimes chose to react violently. Why do you think they do this? What do you think it does to them in the process?

- Can you think of times when you have been confronted by those who are different to you and felt threatened by this? In what way were they different? Can you identify why you felt threatened?

- What is it about difference which sometimes makes us feel that the other people were less human?

Read this story:

An upbringing in the comparative safety of Hertfordshire is hardly the background you would expect from a football hooligan.

But Wells was first taken to Chelsea Football Club as a youngster, by an uncle who was supposed to be babysitting him at home.

As he grew up, fighting at football matches became a part of life, and something he witnessed week in, week out.

Although he was too young to be involved in any violence, the atmosphere created by the trouble gave him a thrill, a feeling he would carry throughout his 'career' as a hooligan.

In fact, it only took a few years for Wells to move from being a teenager on the outside to getting involved in the world of football violence.

"When I moved up into London I was about 17," he said, "You get the sense of the danger of it all, even though I wasn't really part of it.

"In those days you'd come out the ground and there'd be fighting, literally outside the ground, so you didn't even have to be part of the mob, you could just be part of the crowd exiting the ground and it would just be going off."

In the 'firm':

Gradually, and primarily because of his constant presence on the fringes of trouble, Wells' face became known amongst the local Chelsea hooligans.

He went on to become part of the notorious Chelsea Headhunters - one of the 'firms' which constantly battled their way through the 1970s and the 1980s with the likes of the ICF (West Ham) and the Salford Reds (Manchester United).

For Wells, fighting was a way to vent his frustration with his home life.

He said: "With me it was just escapism because I was living in a bad situation with my step-dad. I couldn't really stand up to him. So when I went to Chelsea it was just like I was escaping from it.

"I could immerse myself in it and take out my frustrations. If there was a fight outside the ground, just get rid of some anger in that."

But it is not that way for everyone: "Some people are in it just for the notoriety of it, some people just love the

fighting. It means different things to different people
really."

Combat 18

He became involved in far-right activities in 1994 through
Chelsea hooliganism - beginning an association with the
extreme neo-nazi group Combat 18.
Throughout the 1990s, Combat 18 was associated with
acts of terrorism and violence, including arson attacks. It
was originally set up to act as "security" for British
National Party meetings.
Wells became a senior figure in the group, but became
increasingly disillusioned after 1999 when a friend was
killed in an internal feud. "I knew I would either end up
dead or be in prison for the rest of my life. I also began
to realise the stupidity of what I was involved in".
Two years ago, Wells began working secretly for the anti-
fascist magazine *Searchlight* as an informer.
While working for *Searchlight*, he travelled with far-right
hooligans to Euro 2000 - where he was deported.
He was also present at the Oldham riot - with other
Combat 18 activists and football hooligans. They had
travelled from around the country in an attempt to
provoke violent retaliation from the town's Asian
community.
Wells had hoped his information would help keep the
two sides apart.

Fresh start

At the end of last year, he went abroad to start a new

life. Wells said: "I still believe some of the things I used to believe in, but I now realise that you can't go around hurting innocent people."

Looking back, he claims that the biggest thrill in hooliganism is achieved not during the fight, but before. "It was the build up, just the crescendo just before it all went off, you know, just that feeling of butterflies in your stomach," he said.

Despite this mentality, Darren has witnessed some horrific incidences of football violence, including stabbings, glassings and people being thrown from bridges.

But again, he maintains that even the sense of fear gave him a buzz.

And it is precisely this joy of being terrified that makes it so difficult to opt out of the spiral of violence.

This is also why Darren pours scorn on the notion of the reformed hooligan, and believes you are a hooligan for life.

"How do you just stop being a hooligan," he said, "I don't think you can. I don't think hooliganism is something that people just fly in and out of.

"Strange as it sounds - I think it is really in your blood, I think it's just like people who can't stop smoking, people who can't stop the drinking or doing drugs."

(From the BBC website *Making a new start*
www.bbc.co.uk)

MASCULINE CREDIBILITY?

In Britain the transition from boyhood to manhood for working class youth was ritualised through obtaining employment and acceptance in an all male atmosphere, under the guidance of their elders, for instance being taken to the local pub for their first beer after a day's work. With the decline of traditional, unskilled industrial occupations as a consequence of globalization, and the ending of exclusively male employment, 'the one surviving facet of masculine credibility that has come down to the current group of young men is the ability to fight, and via that, the ability to hold a reputation'. Football hooliganism is a rite of passage into adulthood - a substitute for the rituals of initiations into manhood of former times.

(Gerald A. Arbuckle *Violence, Society, and the Church,* Liturgical Press, Minnesota)

Read this story:

British soldiers: guilty of Iraqi prisoner abuse

Two British soldiers were convicted Wednesday for the abuse of Iraqi detainees. But no one was punished for forcing the prisoners to pose for simulated sex pictures very similar to those of the American Abu Ghraib scandal.

In a court martial that lasted five weeks and involved a

20-month investigation, Lance Corporal Mark Cooley was convicted of simulating punching a detainee and putting a bound man on the front of a forklift truck.

The most senior of the three accused, Corporal Daniel Kenyon was convicted of aiding and abetting in a beating and of failing to report the incidents in which two naked men were forced to simulate sex and the [abuse involving the] forklift truck.

Earlier in the trial, another soldier, Lance Corporal Darren Larkin, pleaded guilty to assault for stamping on one detainee.

All three are members of the Royal Regiment of Fusiliers. The mistreatment of the Iraqi detainees took place after British troops rounded up looters who were stealing powdered milk from a humanitarian aid depot known as Camp Bread Basket, near the southern Iraqi city of Basra, in May 2003.

The jail terms Cooley and Kenyon could each face is up to two years in prison, and Larkin merely six months. The sentencing is expected on Friday.

But the prosecuting team failed to convict anyone for the worst abuse uncovered: that of forcibly posing some of the detainees in simulated sex acts for trophy photos.

The Iraqi prisoner abuse scandal involving the British soldiers mirrored that of the Abu Ghraib prison scandal which involved U.S. soldiers.

The pictures, which were splashed across newspapers

and websites across the world, came to light after
fusilier Gary Bartlam returned to Britain and took his
films to be developed where the film laboratory workers
alerted the authorities.

(From the website *news@aljazeera.com* downloaded 12
April 2005)

*These stories help us to think about situations in which people
become de-humanized and de-humanize others. Perpetrators and
victims alike are de-humanized and the resultant violence can be
frightening.*

- What do you think are the common features in these
  stories?

- Where is the bad news and where is the good news in
  them?

- Can you think of situations in which you have been
  vulnerable? And in which you have been strong? Did
  you ever feel the urge to walk away?

- Can you think of instances when it is a sign of strength
  to walk away?

- The stories paint a dark picture. Can you think of
  examples in your own locality where what happens
  paints a dark story?

- What would you need to do to bring light to similar
  situations in your own context?

- Think back to the Bible passage and then reflect again

on these stories. How did Jesus maintain his dignity in the Bible story? How can we help people to maintain theirs?

Bringing the session to a close

Gather some newspaper cuttings about sports and about the armed forces. Put these around the room and use them as a focus for prayer.

Close with the following affirmation:

Leader: Let us cherish in our hearts that which we proclaim with our lips:

All: Goodness is stronger than evil
            Love is stronger than hate
            Light is stronger than darkness
            Truth is stronger than lies.

Session 5

Moving on?

So when you are offering your gift at the altar, if you remember that your brother or sister has something against you, leave your gift there before the altar and go; first be reconciled to your brother or sister, and then come and offer your gift.

Matthew 5. 23-24

F 7.30

As you begin:

This is the last session in which the group will be together for this course. So, as you gather for this final time, it would be good to think about what the group study has meant to each of you. Consider what you have learned from each other about overcoming violence and how we might be agents of healing and reconciliation in the community.

What new thoughts have you had since the last session about how healing might be achieved?

When everyone has had a chance to share, then pray:

Prayer

> Almighty God,
> you loved the world so much
> that you sent your Son
> not to condemn the world
> but that through him the world might be saved.
>
> We who are quicker to judge than to bless
> fall silent at the extravagance of your grace.
>
> As we are confronted again
> with the depth of human wickedness
> and the greater depth
> of your divine compassion,
> may we not remain unmoved.
> As Christ's arms are stretched out

and his body lifted up,
may we confess our part in the sin of the world,
repent of it,
know the reality of your forgiveness and be transformed.
Amen

Book of Common Order, Saint Andrew Press

In the last session we looked at how violence can dehumanize the victim and the perpetrator. We also began to think about how we could be bringers of light in dark situations.

Purpose

In this session we will look at the aftermath of violence and how to move on.

To think about and discuss

Can you recall times when it has been necessary for you to make a new start in life? What kind of event caused this? (For example: moving home, starting a job or being made redundant, the ending of a relationship, or retirement. For some people a new start might be caused by bereavement). Do you think that the new start happening through choice or through force of circumstance makes a difference to how people react? In what ways?

If you have examples of new starts in your own life, did the new start mean that you left the old behind? What happened?

A 7.45

Bible passage

The burial of Jesus

Read this passage aloud

There were also women looking on from a distance;
among them were Mary Magdalene, and Mary the
mother of James the younger and of Joses, and Salome.
These used to follow him and provided for him when he
was in Galilee; and there were many other women who
had come up with him to Jerusalem.

When evening had come, and since it was the day of
Preparation, that is, the day before the Sabbath, Joseph
of Arimathea, a respected member of the council, who
was also himself waiting expectantly for the kingdom of
God, went boldly to Pilate and asked for the body of
Jesus. Then Pilate wondered if he were already dead;
and summoning the centurion, he asked him whether he
had been dead for some time. When he learned from the
centurion that he was dead, he granted the body to
Joseph. Then Joseph bought a linen cloth, and taking
down the body, wrapped it in the linen cloth, and laid it
in a tomb that had been hewn out of the rock. He then
rolled a stone against the door of the tomb. Mary
Magdalene and Mary the mother of Joses saw where the
body was laid.

Mark 15.40-47

Discuss together:

- Who are the main characters in this passage?

- Where, if anywhere, is the violence in this passage?

- How does this passage make you feel?

F
4.05

Some thoughts about the passage

Again, you might like to ask different members of the group to read different paragraphs.

In terms of telling the gospel story in our worship at this season, we may find ourselves emphasizing Jesus' death on the cross and his resurrection. Many of us do not pay much attention to the part of the story in between. Yet this is a significant moment. It emphasizes that Jesus is completely dead and buried – for without that awful reality there can be no resurrection. That does not mean that we forget his life and his dying – far from it. We have to allow Jesus to be dead; otherwise resurrection can have no reality for us.

One of the points of agreement of all the gospels is that Joseph of Arimathea took responsibility for the body of Jesus. It must have taken some boldness to approach Pilate for permission. It might have been less provocative just to let the Romans do what they would normally do in the circumstances. However, for the observance of religious practice, Jesus should be buried. In death, if not in dying, Jesus was to be given dignity and respect.

Questions for further discussion:

- Do members of the group have stories to tell, from their experience or from people they know, or stories they have heard, of healing coming out of violence?

- What might these stories help us to learn about changing behaviour and overcoming violence?

- How can we help those who have been the victims of violence to have dignity?

A 8. 20

THE TRUTH AND RECONCILIATION COMMISSION

South Africa's story of moving on 'could never be a simple question of forgiveness'... the tens of thousands of victims of torture and the families of dead comrades could not agree to sweep the horrors of the past under the carpet. (Nelson Mandela and) the African National Congress (ANC) had to find a way to forgive without forgetting. The result was Mandela's launch ... in February 1996 of the Truth and Reconciliation Commission.

The ANC wanted to avoid a trial of war criminals like that of the Nazis at the Nuremberg trials, which could create martyrs. ANC lawyers looked at other models in Eastern Europe, Chile and Argentina, and came up with their own solution, 'between amnesty and amnesia'. The Truth Commission, unlike the Latin American investigations, would have quasi judicial powers to grant individual amnesties, with subpoena powers and hearings in public. But applicants for amnesty would have to come out with the full truth. The Truth Commission was thus able to reveal a much more detailed and credible picture ... of what happened.

(Anthony Samson, *Mandela: the authorised biography*, HarperCollins)

Read these stories:

Rwanda

Genocide left Rwanda with a vulnerable and traumatised people who need special attention and care and yet the country has no resources to deal with the situation...

We inherited a devastated economy and a shattered infrastructure that cost a fortune to develop.
...our Government believes that future Genocides can only be avoided by building a strong Nation, a foundation that gives people hope. This can only be a foundation built on Unity, Justice, Human Rights, and Development. It is then and only then that we can talk of healing our people and comfortably say NEVER AGAIN.

We are aware that the way is long, some may tire and rest a little, others will abandon. Our message is always that together we can achieve a lot.

(From a speech by HE Mrs Rosemary Museminali: *Rwanda Seven Years after Genocide: Challenges and Progress to Date*)

Stephen Lawrence

Ten years ago few outside his circle of friends and family knew the name of Stephen Lawrence. Yesterday, at St Martin-in-the-Fields, ministers and senior police officers joined others to remember his lost life and promise. ...
The teenager, who dreamed of becoming an architect, became an icon. The message from speakers was that much had been achieved in his name, but so much more remains: "Over the last 10 years Stephen's name has become synonymous with the battle against the forces that would dehumanise us all, black and white," said David Cruise, formerly of the church where Mrs Lawrence and her husband, Neville, used to take their children.
The service marked the 10th anniversary since a racist gang stabbed Stephen, 18, at a south-east London bus stop. The killers still walk free after a bungled police investigation, labelled "institutionally racist" by a public inquiry.
His parents, ignored for years, fought a gruelling battle to have the police held to account for their mistakes and win promises of change from the government.
In a message read to the congregation, Tony Blair praised their campaign: "They have worked tirelessly to improve race relations in this country and to ensure our society learns the lessons from the senseless murder of their talented son, Stephen."
The Lawrences are the family around whom the recent history of racial inequality in Britain has flowed, and as it touched them, they changed it.

(From an article by Vikram Dodd, the Guardian 23 April 2003)

Forgiving the enemies who jailed him

> Mandela had become famous above all as the man who forgave the enemies who jailed him. ... When Niel Barnard retired as Head of Intelligence, Mandela gave a dinner party for him in Pretoria, with guests including General Willemse, the former Commander of Robben Island. Then 'It doesn't happen in everyone's lifetime,' said Willemse, much moved. 'It's a wonderful experience to live through'.
>
> (Anthony Samson, *Mandela: the authorised biography* HarperCollins)

These stories are about how positive things can come out of terrible tragedy. About how violence and death can be transformed.

- Joseph of Arimathea enabled Jesus to be buried with dignity – he helped the story to move on. Who are the agents of change in the stories above?

- In what situations in your area might you be able to be agents of change?

- Where in the Bible passage, or in any of the others that we have considered, do you find God?

- Do you feel differently about God having looked at these Bible passages from the perspective of this Lent course?

- Do you feel that you know God any better?

- Think back over the previous sessions and consider, if you had to choose a priority for action out of all the issues that have been considered, which would it be?

- Will you take action? How? When? Can you commit yourselves as a group to this or can some of you commit yourselves to action and others to prayer?

Bringing the session and the course to a close

Close the session with prayer for those who have been victims of violence and for those who have been violent to others. Pray for healing and forgiveness for them. Then pray for each other and for your celebrations of Easter. As you pray ask for God's blessing on each other and on your journeys of faith.

Close with the following affirmation:

Leader: Let us cherish in our hearts that which we proclaim with our lips:

All: Goodness is stronger than evil
                 Love is stronger than hate
                 Light is stronger than darkness
                 Truth is stronger than lies.

Reader Evaluation

And now over to you...

CTBI and the authors of this book would very much like to know how this course has been for you. We would be grateful if you would return this questionnaire by 31 July 2006, either by cutting it out of this book, or by photocopying it and sending it to:

Lent Course Evaluation 2006
CTBI
Bastille Court
2 Paris Garden
London SE1 8ND.

1. I read this book ~~on my own~~/ as part of a church group.

2. Our group had .....12..... members.

3. The following denominations were represented:

Church of Scotland
Roman Catholic
Scottish Episcopal

4. What county or major town are you situated in?

CUPAR, FIFE

5. What were the good points about the course?

*Very well constructed
—it flowed well*

6. What were the weaknesses of the course?

*had to be timed carefully
(not really a weakness)*

7. Are there any outcomes from doing this course? *e.g.
starting a community project, supporting a charity or
cause, praying in a more informed way, developing
friendships, etc.?*

*friendships — otherwise many of us
are pleased we are in an ecumenical*

8. Your name and address *(optional – please feel free to
remain anonymous if you so wish)*   *Justice & Peace
group*

9. I would/ I would not like to be placed on the mailing
list for CTBI Publications

10. I would like to receive information from CTBI by
email: *(please write your email address here)*

Fiona Gordon

machrie@madasafish . com

*I found this an unusual angle for reading the
Pass in story. Very refreshing & meaningful
in today's world, Thank you so much*

About the Authors

Myra Blyth is a Baptist minister and former Deputy General Secretary of the Baptist Union of Great Britain and Ireland. She is currently a lecturer at Regent's Park College Oxford, teaching liturgy and ecumenical studies. Myra is researching issues related to overcoming violence.

Wendy Robins is the Director of Communications and Resources for the Anglican Diocese of Southwark. An experienced author and editor, she has worked on many international and ecumenical projects, particularly relating to women's issues and the church. Wendy is an Anglican priest.

Acknowledgements

The authors wish to thank the Church Life committee for their input into this publication, and Steve Whiting of the Religious Society of Friends (Quakers) for writing the introduction. Thanks are also due to the Lent Review Group whose names are listed below:

Bishop Joe Aldred – Church of God of Prophecy
Mrs Sally Beaumont – Church of Scotland
Revd Anthony Clarke – Baptist Union of Great Britain
Major Alan Dixon – Salvation Army
Revd Rowena Francis – United Reformed Church
Bede Gerrard – Orthodox Church
Helen Hood – Scottish Episcopalian Church
Elizabeth Ingram – Church of England
John Johansen-Berg – United Reformed Church
Elisabeth Shend'ge – Society of Friends
Carys Whelan – Roman Catholic Church

Fr Colin Carr and Mrs Bernadette Askins and the NE Ecumenical Group for trialling the course.

And CTBI staff as below:
Dr David Goodbourn

Revd Judith Maizel-Long
Mr Paul Renshaw
Ms Katrina Bradley

Every effort has been made to trace ownership and verify the accuracy of the material quoted in this book. The publishers will gladly rectify any error or omission in future editions. We wish to thank the following for permission to reproduce the extracts below:

Session One

Bridging the Gap, Greyfriars Centre, 270 Ballater St, Glasgow, G5 UYT, e-mail secretary@bridging-the-gap.org
Journeying through Conflict – part of life from the Baptist Training Pack *Handling Tensions in Church Relationships* – Vivienne Lassetter and Ernie Whalley, March 2004, Baptist Union of Great Britain
A Volcano in my Tummy – Helping children to handle anger, Elaine Whitehouse and Warick Pudney, 1996 ISBN 0-86571-349-9 New Society Publishers, Canada
Marcus Armstrong, an extract from his journal reproduced with permission.
John Johansen-Berg, Founder of the Community for Reconciliation
A Wee Worship Book © 1999 Wild Goose Resource Group, Iona Community Glasgow G2 3DH

Session Two

Justice and Peace: a restorative response to crime by Martin Wright, printed in The Bridge (the Southwark Diocesan Newspaper October 2002). Martin Wright is author of *Restoring Respect for Justice* (Waterside Press 1999) and is a board member of the European Forum for Restorative Justice.
A Place of Redemption, Catholic Bishops' Conference of England and Wales

Rethinking Sentencing Tim Newall, Church House Publishing
Sin and Forgiveness Kay Carmichael, Ashgate Gower House

Session Three

Johnston McMaster, quoted from his paper given at the CTBI
Conference *Beyond Violence* (2004) Swanwick.
I was part of it, I killed your father Simon Fanshawe, 13 October 2004
© Guardian Newspapers Limited 2004.
The Art of Forgiveness Geiko Muller-Fahrenholz, World Council of
Churches

Session Four

Violence, Society and the Church Gerald A Arbuckle, Liturgical Press,
Minnesota,
BBC News at bbcnews.co.uk, *Making a New Start* downloaded 7 April
2005
Al Jazeera news agency, downloaded from www.aljazeera.com
downloaded 12 April 2005

Session Five

Mandela - the Authorised Biography reprinted by permission of
HarperCollins Publishers Ltd, © Anthony Samson, 1999
HE Mrs Rosemary Museminali, from *Rwanda Seven Years after
Genocide: Challenges and Progress to Date*, an address given by Her
Excellency the Ambassador.
Stephen Lawrence mourners pledge to carry on the fight Vikram Dodd,
23 April 2003 © *Guardian Newspapers Unlimited*.